My
Gulf world
and me

Activity Book

Level 4

by **Helen M Thomson**

WAYS LEARNING

PEARSON

Published by Pearson Education Limited,
Edinburgh Gate, Harlow, Essex, CM20 2JE.

Text © Pearson Education Limited 2013

Edited by Kim Vernon
Designed by Juice Creative
Original illustrations © Pearson Education 2013
Illustrated by John Batten (Beehive illustration),
Gareth Clarke and Juice
Cover design by Juice
Cover photo © FotoLibra
Cover illustration by Gareth Clarke

First published 2013

ARP impression 98

British Library Cataloguing in Publication Data
A catalogue record for this book is available from
the British Library.

ISBN 978 0 435 15193 5

Printed in the UK by Ashford Colour Press Ltd

Acknowledgements
The author and publisher would like to thank
the following individuals and organisations for
permission to reproduce photographs:
(Key: b-bottom; c-centre; l-left; r-right; t-top)

Fotolia.com: 1 (bird), 1 (deer), 1 (falcon), 1 (fox),
1 (lion), 1 (lizard), 1 (mouse), 1 (rabbit), 2c, 3br, 4b, 8tr,
8cr, 8bl, 8br, 9l, 10tl, 10tr, 10bl, 10br, 13 (black car),
13 (blue car), 13 (red car), 13 (yellow car), 13c, 15tl, 15tr,
15cl, 15cr, 15bl, 15br, 18 (glue), 18 (paints), 18 (scissors),
18 (toothbrush), 18 (water), 20tl, 20tr, 20bl;
Glow Images: 20br;
Shutterstock.com: 6c, 18 (black paper)

All other images © Pearson Education

Every effort has been made to contact copyright
holders of material reproduced in this book. Any
omissions will be rectified in subsequent printings if
notice is given to the publishers.

Contents

Fantastic falcons

A falcon is a bird of prey. This means it is a predator.

Some of the animals here are predators and some of them are prey.

Circle the predators and draw lines to the animals they eat (their prey). There may be several lines to the same prey.

I

Fantastic falcons

Label the parts of the falcon. Choose from the words below.

strong legs   talons   feathered tail

strong eyes   sharp, hooked beak

2

Fantastic falcons

Are these sentences true or false?
If they are false, write the correct sentence underneath.

The first one is done for you.

1 Falcons fly very slowly.

<u>X false</u>

<u>Falcons fly very fast.</u>

2 Falconry has been a tradition in the Gulf for thousands of years. _____

_____

3 A hood is placed over the head of a falcon when it is flying. _____

_____

4 A falconer wears a glove to protect his hands and arms from the bird's talons.

_____

_____

5 It takes two to four weeks to train a falcon. _____

_____

6 Falcons hunt mostly during the day. _____

_____

7 Falcons only eat reptiles.

_____

_____

8 Falcons nest in high places.

_____

_____

3

Fantastic falcons

Find these words in *Fantastic falcons*.
Look through the reader and when you find
the word write down the page number.

incubation

page 13 _____

habitat

_____

binoculars

_____

equipment

_____

thousands

_____

falconry

_____

wingspan

_____

magnify

_____

peregrine

_____

migrate

_____

prey

_____

survive

_____

Some words appear more
than once.

Fantastic falcons

Read the following sentence out loud to your friend.
Read it as fast as you can!

*Five feathered falcons flying fast found four fat,
furry foxes fighting for food.*

Draw a picture of the five falcons and the four foxes below.

Can you make up more sentences like this one?

5

Buildings in the Gulf

Name the features of the mosque.
Choose from the words below.

crescent   arches   pillars

minaret   domed roof

6

Buildings in the Gulf

Find the answers to these questions.
The first one is done for you.

1 Why do Muslims go to the mosque?

To pray

2 What can you find on the floor of a mosque?

_____

3 Why were the walls of forts built high and thick?

_____

4 Name three things that you can buy at a souk.

_____

5 What is the name of the art of beautiful writing?

_____

6 Why were wind towers built?

_____

Buildings in the Gulf

Where would you do these things? Match the activity to the place. The first one is done for you.

pray

pour hot date juice on your enemies

shop

sleep in a cool place

the souk

a fort

a wind tower

a mosque

Buildings in the Gulf

Complete the other half of this pattern so that it is symmetrical.

Use a mirror to help you.

Buildings in the Gulf

Look at these pictures.

Draw the line of symmetry in each picture.
The first one is done for you.

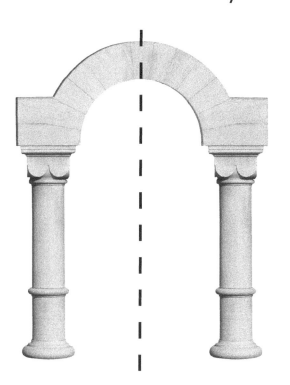

A tour around the Gulf!

Write an interesting sentence about each of
the following places.

Al Areen Wildlife Park
_____
_____
_____

Al Jilali and Al Mirani
forts
_____
_____
_____

Manama Souk
_____
_____
_____

The Museum of
Islamic Art
_____
_____
_____

The Kuwait Towers
_____
_____
_____

Kingdom Centre
Riyadh
_____
_____
_____

Ras Al Jinz Beach
_____
_____
_____

Jebel Hafeet in Al Ain
_____
_____
_____

A tour around the Gulf!

Look at the chart. It shows the size of the populations of six Gulf countries.

Look through *A tour around the Gulf!* and write the names of the countries.

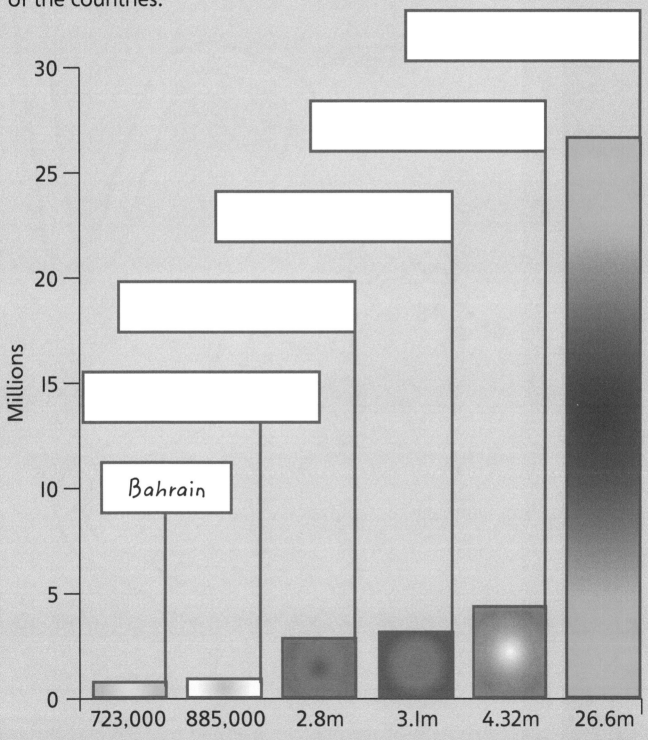

Millions

30

25

20

15

10 — Bahrain

5

0

723,000   885,000   2.8m   3.1m   4.32m   26.6m

A tour around the Gulf!

In Qatar, there is a race track called Losail International Circuit.

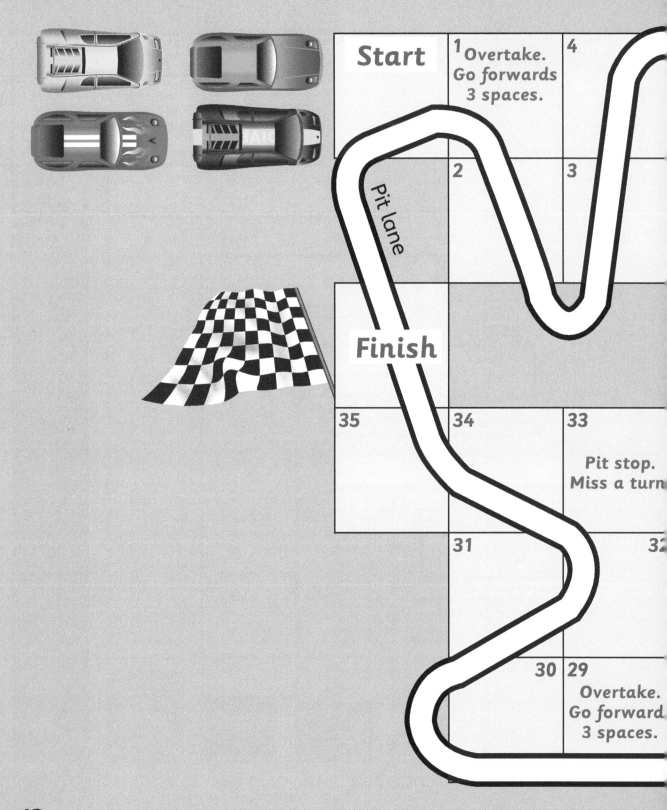

Start

1 Overtake. Go forwards 3 spaces.

4

Pit lane

2

3

Finish

35

34

33

Pit stop. Miss a turn

31

32

30 | 29

Overtake. Go forward 3 spaces.

Use the race track below to race your friends to the finish line.

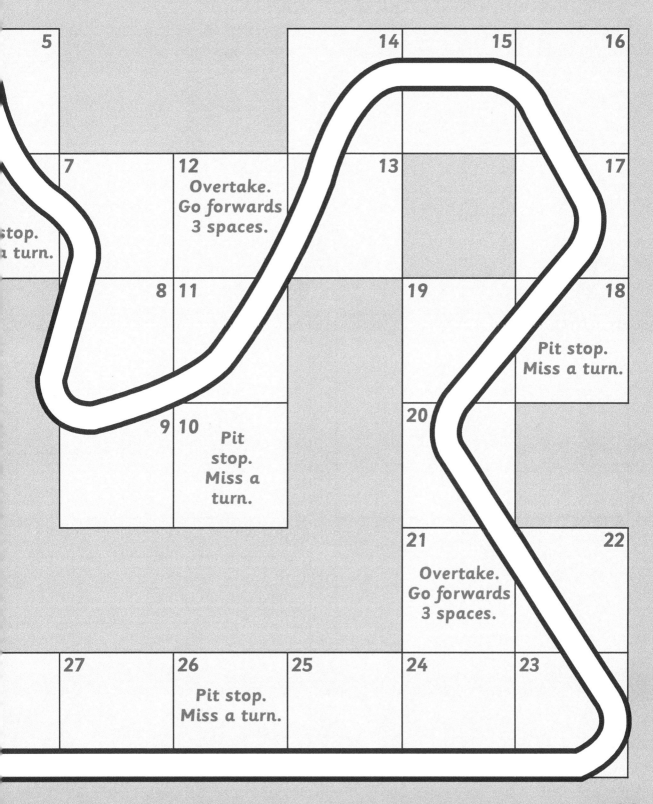

5

14 15 16

7 12
**Overtake.
Go forwards
3 spaces.**

13 17

stop.
a turn.

8 11

19 18

**Pit stop.
Miss a turn.**

9 10
**Pit
stop.
Miss a
turn.**

20

21 22

**Overtake.
Go forwards
3 spaces.**

27 26 25 24 23

**Pit stop.
Miss a turn.**

A tour around the Gulf!

These are the flags of the countries in the Gulf.
Colour them in using the correct colours.
Look through *A tour around the Gulf!* to find
the correct colours.

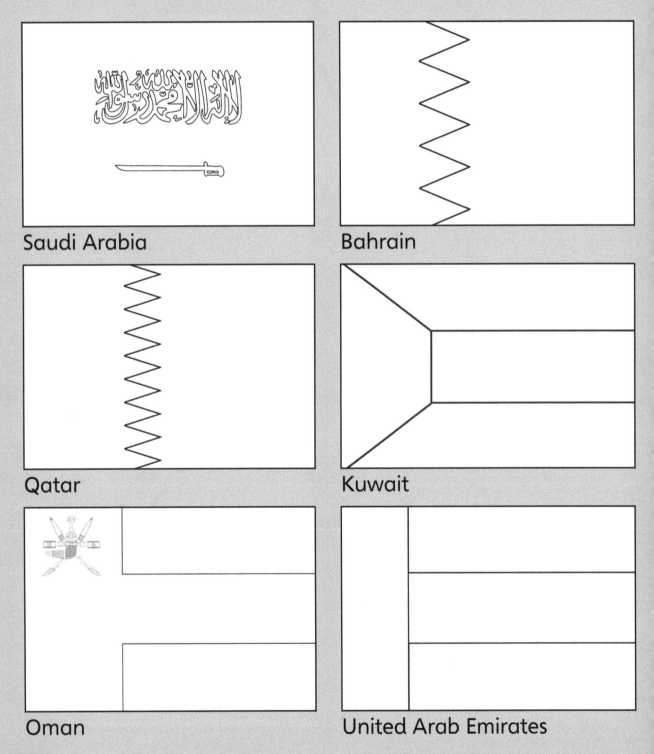

Saudi Arabia

Bahrain

Qatar

Kuwait

Oman

United Arab Emirates

Creating a night skyline

These words all contain the same sound.

It is spelled in a different way in each word.

night   sky   line

Read these words with your teacher and then write them in the correct column.

bright	mine	fly	light	life
eye	fight	survive	flight	fine
try	side	write	sigh	

igh	y	i–e
night	sky	line

Creating a night skyline

Draw a city skyline.

Draw a desert skyline.

Draw a souk skyline.

17

Creating a night skyline

Write a list of all the materials you need to
create a night skyline. Here are some of them.

List

Creating a night skyline

Find words in the word search that mean:

1 Well known _____

2 To do something again _____

3 The image of something
seen in a mirror _____

4 New and recent _____

5 Not the same _____

6 Something made from or
which looks like metal _____

7 A way or method of doing
or making something _____

d	i	f	f	e	r	e	n	t	v
g	i	f	a	m	o	u	s	p	f
r	e	f	l	e	c	t	i	o	n
s	a	t	c	m	o	d	e	r	n
u	t	e	c	h	n	i	q	u	e
p	m	e	t	a	l	l	i	c	y
v	r	q	r	e	p	e	a	t	l

Deserts

How do these animals survive in the desert?
Make notes about the special features and habits
that help them to survive.

The first one is done for you.

jerboa

fennec fox

Gets water from food

Burrows underground to escape heat

Has big eyes to see in the dark

Has long hind legs

camel

spiny-tailed lizard

20

Deserts

You are going sand driving in the desert.
Make a list of the things you will need. Here are
some suggestions. Can you think of any others?

List

_____

_____

_____

_____

_____

_____

_____

_____

Deserts

Fill in the missing words. Choose from the words below.

Deserts in the Gulf are _____ and _____ .

They are _____ places to live in but the Bedouin

people knew how to _____ in the desert. The Bedouin

people lived in _____ and kept _____ .

Other animals such as _____ , _____ and

_____ live in the desert. They have _____

features to help them to survive.

camels	hot	jerboas	dry	survive
foxes	special	tents	difficult	lizards

22

Deserts

Look at the pictures of deserts in the reader *Deserts*.
How many different shades of brown, yellow and
orange can you see?

Look at how the light makes shades on the dunes. Use brown,
, orange and red pencils to colour in this desert picture.

23

Teaching notes

Introduction

The following notes provide suggestions for maximising learning opportunities when using Activity Book Level 4 of the *My Gulf world and me* series. The book is designed to provide multi-sensory and varied activities to encourage the children to practise the target language in enjoyable ways. It is important to remember that young children learn through doing. They are much more likely to remember what they are taught if the lesson is fun. It is also important to remember that all children learn at different rates and in different ways. For example, some children may need extra help to complete the reading and writing activities. This will be the case if they have not yet been taught English phonemes and letter-to-sound associations.

A sense of success for all children should be incorporated into the lesson to develop the self-confidence of each child. Good self-esteem and confidence are essential to learning. A child who lacks self-confidence will be reluctant to practise new language in case they fail.

All learners of a second language need to hear and practise the target language several times before they will remember it. So include as many opportunities as possible to do this through games and songs.

Fantastic falcons

Activity 1
Introduce the word 'predator' to the children and explain that it means an animal that hunts and eats other smaller animals. Name the animals in the pictures: fox, falcon, rabbit, mouse, lion, gazelle, bird, lizard – and talk about which are predators and which are prey. Explain that some of the predators have more than one type of prey, and that sometimes animals that are predators of small animals may themselves become prey for larger animals.

Activity 2
Look at the picture of the falcon with the children and talk about the following features: strong legs, talons, feathered tail, strong eyes, sharp hooked beak, and why a falcon needs these things. If possible, organise a visit to a falconry centre or arrange for a falconer to bring falcons to the school.

Activity 3
Read the sentences with the children to make sure that they understand them. Encourage children to refer to the reader to find the answers. They will be able to 'lift' most of the answers from the text but some questions, for example question 4, extend their comprehension skills by requiring them to use additional vocabulary.

Activity 4
Go through the following words with the children to ensure that they understand the meaning: 'incubation', 'habitat', 'binoculars', 'equipment', 'thousands', 'falconry', 'wingspan', 'magnify', 'peregrine', 'migrate', 'prey' and 'survive'. Don't expect them to be able to spell all the words and not all children will remember the meanings. Ask them to look through the reader as quickly as they can to locate the words. Scanning text to find specific items is an important skill for children to develop.

Activity 5
Alliteration is a good way to reinforce phonemes and graphemes where the children need extra practice. Introduce these through tongue twisters. You could also write this tongue twister on the board: 'She sells seashells on the seashore.' Encourage them to create tongue twisters of their own.

Buildings in the Gulf

Activity 1
Recap on the names of the architectural features of a mosque. The children should choose the correct words to write in the blank spaces. Help those who need extra support by writing the initial letter in the space. If possible, bring in a 3-D model of a mosque to demonstrate the features more clearly.

Activity 2
This comprehension activity involves higher-level reading skills as the children cannot find the answers by simply 'lifting' the sentence from the text. It is important to support them and ensure that they understand the text in the reader.

Activity 3
Before they complete the activity, tell the children to look in their reader to find where the following activities take place, either now or in the past: praying, pouring a hot mixture of date juice on your enemies, shopping and sleeping in a cool place. They should draw a line from the activity to the location where it might take place.

Activity 4
Provide the children with small mirrors and explore the idea of symmetry of objects. Provide them with coloured pencils to complete the symmetrical shapes in the picture. It should be noted that many natural objects, such as a camel or a falcon, are bilaterally symmetrical from side to side, but are not symmetrical from top to bottom. Other objects, such as a daisy flower or a tomato, have radial symmetry when viewed from on top. Discuss some of these ideas about symmetry with the children.

Activity 5
Elicit the names of the objects from the children: archway, car, dome, butterfly – and talk about which ones are symmetrical, and about which axis they are symmetrical, before the children complete the activity.

A tour around the Gulf!

Activity 1
Ask the children to search *A tour around the Gulf!* to find an interesting fact about each of the following places: Al Areen Wildlife Park, Manama Souk, the Kuwait Towers, Ras al Jinz Beach, Al Jilali and Al Mirani, the Museum of Islamic Art, the Kingdom Centre Riyadh and Jebel Hafeet in Al Ain. Read through the text to ensure that the children understand it before they complete the activity. Refer them to the symbols of the places as visual prompts to locate the relevant paragraphs.

Activity 2
Look at the graph with the children. If they are unfamiliar with bar charts, explain how these are used to represent and compare figures and information. Demonstrate how bar charts might be used to represent figures that are relevant to the children such as the sizes of the classes in their school. Encourage them to scan the reader to find the statistical information they need to label each bar on the chart.

Activity 3
Arrange the children in pairs or groups of three. Provide each group with dice and a different-coloured counter for each child. This is designed to be a fun activity that children of all ability levels can participate in. For an extension activity, refer to the flashcard showing the racing car and introduce related vocabulary, for example wheels, tyres, headlights and hub caps. Explain the meaning of 'pit stop' and 'overtake'.

Activity 4
Look at the flags with the children and explain that they must choose the correct colours and colour the flags in. Remind them to look through the reader to find the correct colours.

Creating a night skyline

Activity 1
Write 'igh', 'y' and 'i-e' on the board and point out to the children that they all make the sound 'ie'. Read the words from the activity book to the children, and then ask them to write the words in the correct column under the corresponding spelling.

Activity 2
Look at the skylines in the reader and encourage the children to draw their own.

Activity 3
Using the flashcards, revise the names of the following objects with the children: pencil, scissors, large sheet of black paper, toothbrush, bottle of PVA glue, card, wide sheet of paper, blue pencil crayon, glitter, gold and silver marker pens, metallic crayons, paint tray, paint, pot of water, sticky tack. Ask them to complete the list. Tell them that they can use their reader to find the correct spellings.

Activity 4
Ask the children to look in the glossary of the reader to find the definitions of the words they will be looking for in the word search. More able pupils will be able to work on this independently. Other children will need help. The words are: 'different', 'famous', 'reflection', 'modern', 'technique', 'metallic', 'repeat'.

Deserts

Activity 1
Read through the information with the children about the desert animals on pages 6 and 7 of the reader and check that they understand. Tell them to reread independently and identify the parts of the text that refer to how the animals survive in the desert. Show them how to make notes to record this information. Scanning for specific information and making succinct notes is an important literacy skill.

Activity 2
Use the flashcards to talk about the things needed for a trip to the desert. Ask the children to compile a list. Refer them to page 10 of the reader to find the correct spellings if they are unable to spell the words independently.

Activity 3
Go through the cloze activity text with the children to ensure that they understand it before they complete the activity, selecting from the words at the bottom of the page: 'camels', 'hot', 'jerboas', 'dry', 'survive', 'foxes', 'special', 'tents', 'difficult' and 'lizards'.

Activity 4
Look at pictures of the desert and the different formations of sand dunes in the reader and use flashcards to help emphasise the words. Draw the children's attention to the different shades and the shapes created by shadow and light. Encourage them to experiment in creating light and shadow effects with pencil crayons. You could also provide yellow, orange, brown and red paints and larger pieces of paper to give them the opportunity to create this on a larger scale.

الصحارى

النشاط ١
اقرأ المعلومات مع الأطفال بعناية عن حيوانات الصحراء في الصفحتين ٦ و ٧ من كتاب القراءة، وتأكد من استيعابهم. اطلب منهم إعادة القراءة بمفردهم وقم بتحديد أجزاء النص التي توضح الكيفية التي تتمكن من خلالها الحيوانات من البقاء على قيد الحياة في الصحراء. ووضح لهم كيفية تدوين ملاحظات لتسجيل هذه المعلومات. يعد البحث عن معلومات معينة وتقديم ملاحظات موجزة مهارة مهمة تتعلق بمعرفة القراءة والكتابة.

النشاط ٢
استخدم البطاقات التعليمية للحديث عن الأشياء المطلوبة للقيام برحلة إلى الصحراء. اطلب من الأطفال عمل قائمة. قم بإحالتهم إلى صفحة ١٠ من كتاب القراءة لمعرفة الهجاء الصحيح للكلمات إذا لم يتمكنوا من كتابة الكلمات بالشكل الصحيح بمفردهم.

النشاط ٣
اقرأ نص نشاط إكمال الناقص مع الأطفال لضمان فهمهم له قبل إكمال النشاط، عن طريق اختيار الكلمات الموجودة أسفل الصفحة: "جمال" (camels)، "ساخن" (hot)، "يرابيع" (jerboas)، "جاف" (dry)، "حياة" (survive)، "ثعالب" (foxes)، "خيام خاصة" (special tents)، "صعب" (difficult)، "سحلية" (lizard).

النشاط ٤
انظر إلى صور الصحراء والتكوينات المختلفة للكثبان الرملية في كتاب القراءة واستخدم البطاقات التعليمية للمساعدة على تأكيد الكلمات. اجذب انتباه الأطفال إلى الظلال والأشكال المختلفة التي تكونها الظلال والأضواء. قم بتشجيع الأطفال على التجربة لعمل تأثيرات بالأضواء والظلال باستخدام الأقلام الرصاص الملونة. كما يمكنك كذلك توفير ألوان صفراء وبرتقالية وبنية وحمراء وأجزاء كبيرة من الورق لمنحهم الفرصة لعمل ذلك على نطاق أوسع.

عمل أفق ليلي

النشاط ١
اكتب "igh" و"y" و"i-e" على السبورة، ووضح للأطفال أنها جميعها تصدر الصوت "ie". اقرأ الكلمات من كتاب النشاط على الأطفال، ثم اطلب منهم كتابة الكلمات في العمود الصحيح تحت الهجاء الصحيح.

النشاط ٢
لقد تم تصميم هذا النشاط لتوفير المزيد من تدريبات القراءة للأطفال لتقوية مهارة قراءة الجمل الكاملة. قم بتشجيعهم على العثور على القسم المناسب في كتاب القراءة الخاص بهم (الصفحتين الثامنة والتاسعة) ثم قراءة الجمل وترقيم الصور بالترتيب الصحيح.

النشاط ٣
باستخدام البطاقات التعليمية، راجع أسماء الأشياء التالية مع الأطفال: قلم رصاص، مقص، ورقة سوداء كبيرة، فرشاة أسنان، عبوة صمغ PVA، بطاقة، ورقة بيضاء، قلم رصاص ملون أزرق اللون، بريق، أقلام تعليم ذهبية وفضية اللون، أقلام ألوان ملونة لامعة، حاوية طلاء، طلاء، إناء ماء، مثبت لاصق. اطلب منهم إكمال القائمة. قل لهم إن بإمكانهم استخدام كتب القراءة الخاصة بهم لمعرفة الهجاء الصحيح.

النشاط ٤
اطلب من الأطفال الاطلاع على قاموس كتاب القراءة لمعرفة تعريفات الكلمات التي يبحثون عنها أثناء البحث عن الكلمات. سوف يتمكن التلاميذ الذين لديهم قدرات أكبر من العمل في هذا النشاط بمفردهم. وسوف يحتاج الأطفال الآخرون إلى المساعدة.

المباني في الخليج

النشاط ١

قم بإيجاز أسماء السمات المعمارية للمسجد. يجب أن يختار الأطفال الكلمات المناسبة لكتابتها في الفراغات. شجع من يحتاجون إلى المزيد من المساعدة من خلال كتابة الحرف الأول في المسافة. إذا أمكن، يمكن إحضار مجسم ثلاثي الأبعاد لمسجد لتوضيح السمات بشكل أكثر وضوحًا.

النشاط ٢

يحتوي هذا النشاط الشامل على مهارات قراءة متطورة المستوى حيث إن الأطفال لا يمكنهم العثور على الإجابات من خلال "نقل" (lifting) العبارات من النص بسهولة. من الضروري مساعدتهم والتأكد من فهمهم للنص الموجود في كتاب القراءة.

النشاط ٣

قبل أن يكمل الطلاب النشاط، اطلب منهم النظر في كتب القراءة الخاصة بهم للعثور على أماكن حدوث الأنشطة التالية، إما الآن وإما في الماضي: إقامة الصلاة، صب خليط ساخن من عصير البلح على الأعداء، التسوق، والنوم في مكان بارد. ويجب أن يقوموا برسم خط بين النشاط والمكان الذي يمكن أن يحدث به.

النشاط ٤

قم بتوفير مرايا صغيرة للأطفال وقم باستكشاف فكرة تماثل الأشياء. قم بإعطاء أقلام رصاص ملونة للأطفال لإكمال الأشكال المتماثلة في الصورة. يجب ملاحظة أن العديد من الأشياء الطبيعية، مثل الجمل أو الصقر، متماثلة بشكل ثنائي من جانب إلى آخر، ولكنها غير متماثلة من أعلى إلى أسفل. وهناك أشياء أخرى، مثل زهرة الأقحوان أو الطماطم، تتشابه بشكل قطري عند النظر إليها من أعلى. ناقش بعضًا من هذه الأفكار عن التماثل مع الأطفال.

النشاط ٥

استنبط أسماء الأشياء من الأطفال. فراشة، سيارة، سمر، وتحدث عما هو متماثل منها، وعن المحاور المتماثلة بها، قبل أن يكملوا النشاط.

جولة حول الخليج!

النشاط ١

شجع الأطفال على البحث في موضوع "جولة حول الخليج!" (A tour around the Gulf!) للوصول إلى حقائق مثيرة للاهتمام حول كل مكان من الأماكن التالية: محمية العرين للحياة البرية، سوق المنامة، أبراج الكويت، شاطئ رأس الجينز، الجلالي والميراني، متحف الفن الإسلامي، مركز المملكة بالرياض. جبل حفيت في مدينة العين. اقرأ النص بعناية للتأكد من أن الأطفال يفهمونه قبل إكمال النشاط. قم بإحالتهم إلى رموز الأماكن كمحفزات مرئية لتحديد أماكن الفقرات المرتبطة بها.

النشاط ٢

انظر إلى الرسم البياني مع الأطفال. إذا لم يكونوا على دراية بالرسوم البيانية الشريطية، اشرح لهم كيفية استخدامها لتمثيل الأرقام والمعلومات ومقارنتها.

وضح كيف يمكن استخدام الرسوم البيانية الشريطية للتعبير عن الأرقام المتعلقة بالأطفال مثل أحجام الفصول في مدرستهم. شجعهم على البحث في كتاب القراءة للعثور على المعلومات الإحصائية التي يحتاجون إليها لتسمية كل شريط في الرسم البياني.

النشاط ٣

قم بترتيب الأطفال في أزواج أو مجموعات من ثلاثة أطفال. قم بإعطاء كل مجموعة نرد وعداد بلون مختلف لكل طفل. الهدف أن يكون هذا النشاط ممتعًا يمكن أن يشارك فيه الأطفال من كافة القدرات. للحصول على نشاط إضافي، ارجع إلى البطاقة التعليمية التي توضح سيارة السباق وقم بتعريف الأطفال الكلمات المرتبطة بها، على سبيل المثال، الإطارات والعجلات والمصابيح الأمامية وأغطية المحاور.

النشاط ٤

انظر مع الأطفال إلى الأعلام واشرح أنه يجب عليهم اختيار الألوان الصحيحة وتلوين الأعلام بها. قم بتذكيرهم بالاطلاع على كتاب القراءة لمعرفة الألوان الصحيحة.

ملاحظات التدريس

المقدمة

توفر الملاحظات التالية اقتراحات للوصول إلى أقصى مدى من فرص التعلم عند استخدام المستوى ٤ من كتاب الأنشطة من سلسلة *My Gulf World and Me series*. وقد تم تصميم هذا الكتاب لتوفير سبل متعددة الحواس ومتنوعة لتشجيع الأطفال على ممارسة اللغة المستهدفة بطرق ممتعة. ومن المهم أن نتذكر أن الأطفال الصغار يتعلمون من خلال الممارسة العملية. ومن الجائز جدًا أن يتذكروا ما يتعلمونه، إذا كان الدرس ممتعًا. كما أنه من المهم أن نتذكر أن كل الأطفال يتعلمون بمعدلات مختلفة وبطرق مختلفة. فعلى سبيل المثال، قد يحتاج بعض الأطفال إلى مساعدة إضافية لاستكمال أنشطة القراءة والكتابة. وسيكون هذا هو الحال إذا لم يكونوا قد عُلّموا طريقة نطق الكلمات في اللغة الإنجليزية وارتباط الحرف بالصوت الصوت.

يجب أن يتضمن الدرس الإحساس بالنجاح لدى جميع الأطفال لتعزيز ثقة كل طفل بنفسه. ويُعد الاعتزاز الجيد بالنفس والثقة ضرورة للتعلم. فالطفل الذي تنقصه الثقة بالنفس سيصبح مترددًا في ممارسة اللغة الجديدة في حال فشله.

ويحتاج جميع المتعلمين للغة ثانية إلى سماع اللغة المستهدفة وممارستها عدة مرات قبل أن يحفظوها. ولذلك، قم بإتاحة أكبر عدد ممكن من الفرص لأداء ذلك من خلال الألعاب والأغاني.

الصقور الرائعة

النشاط ١

قم بتعريف الأطفال على كلمة "مفترس" (predator) وقم بشرح أنها تعني الحيوان الذي يصطاد ويأكل الحيوانات الأخرى الصغرى. قم بتسمية الحيوانات الموجودة في الصورة: صقر، أرنب، فأر، أسد، غزال، ثعلب، طائر، وتكلم عما هو منها من الحيوانات المفترسة وما هو من الفرائس. اشرح أن بعض الحيوانات المفترسة تفترس أكثر من نوع من الفرائس، وأنه في بعض الأحيان يمكن أن تكون الحيوانات التي تفترس حيوانات صغيرة هي نفسها فريسة لحيوانات أكبر.

النشاط ٢

انظر إلى صورة الصقر مع الأطفال وتحدث عن الصفات التالية: ساقين قويتين، ومخالب، وذيل به ريش، وعينين قويتين، ومنقار معقوف حاد، وسبب حاجة الصقر إلى هذه الأشياء. إذا كان بالإمكان، قم بتنظيم زيارة إلى مركز للصقور أو قم بالترتيب مع أحد العاملين في مجال الصقور لإحضار صقور إلى المدرسة.

النشاط ٣

اقرأ العبارات مع الأطفال للتأكد من فهمهم لها. شجع الأطفال على الرجوع إلى كتب القراءة للعثور على الإجابات. وسوف يتمكنون من "الحصول على" (lift) معظم الإجابات من النص، إلا أن بعض الأسئلة، على سبيل المثال السؤال الرابع، يزيد من مهارات الفهم الخاصة بهم من خلال مطالبتهم باستخدام كلمات إضافية.

النشاط ٤

قم بالمرور على الكلمات التالية مع الأطفال لضمان فهمهم معناها: "الحضانة" (incubation)، و"الموطِن" (habitat)، و"المنظار" (binoculars)، و"المعدات" (equipment)، و"آلاف" (thousands)، و"تربية الصقور" (falconry)، و"المسافة بين الجناحين" (wingspan)، و"تكبير" (magnify)، و"القطامي نوع من الصقور" (peregrine)، و"هجرة" (migrate)، و"فريسة" (prey)، و"حياة" (survive). لا تتوقع منهم التمكن من هجاء كل الكلمات، ولن يتذكر كل الأطفال المعاني. اطلب منهم الاطلاع على كتاب القراءة بسرعة قدر الإمكان لتحديد أماكن الكلمات. فالبحث في النص للعثور على عناصر معينة مهارة مهمة تجب تنميتها لدى الأطفال.

النشاط ٥

تكرار الحرف طريقة جيدة لتقوية القدرة على معرفة الحروف، عند حاجة الأطفال إلى المزيد من التدريب. قم بتعريف الأطفال عليها من خلال عبارات صعبة النطق. كما يمكنك كذلك كتابة العبارات صعبة النطق على السبورة: "إنها تبيع صدف البحر على شاطئ البحر" (She sells seashells on the seashore) شجع الأطفال على إنشاء العبارات صعبة النطق الخاصة بهم.